ATHENA to ZEUS

A–Z of Mediterranean Cooking

STEPHANIE PATSALIS
contributing authors
Athena Patsalis & Eleni Patalis

Athena to Zeus
A–Z of Mediterranean Cooking

ISBN 978-0-578-77579-1

Dedication

Thankful to God
My yiayia—Asimina
My children—Athena & Eleni
My niece and nephews—Bobby, Danny & Sylvia
My Godchildren—
Eleni, Claire, Josephine, Lukas, Matthew, Nikos. Sydney, Kobe and Andy Villalongo
Marian Class of 2020

Acknowledgments

Food Photography by Mike Howard
Contributing authors and editors
Athena Patsalis
Eleni Patsalis
Hair and Makeup by Ellie Ringler
Portion of the proceeds to H.A.F.F.

Contents

Contents

Entrees

Sweets & Treats

Introduction

The idea for the Athena to Zeus Cookbook sprouted with a growing desire to bring Stephanie Patsalis' Mediterranean recipes to family-friendly character concepts inspired by Greek Mythology. Stephanie wanted to champion cooking as an essential life skill, and inspire children and families to embark on a voyage into the kitchen together.

A playbook of hands-on-fun recipes, the Athena to Zeus is merely the beginning of a sensory exploration into the world of fresh ingredients. By summoning the senses of smell, touch, and taste, the reader becomes a culinary creator and inventor on an adventure that can be savored as much in taste as it is in the heart and mind.

We'll take you to the tippy top of Mount Olympus over the Greek Isles and into the hearts and minds of the Greek gods. Let this be your personal invitation to dig into culinary adventure. Gather your family for a cooking project. Whether you're in search of an appetizer for your next gathering, a main dish, a special Sunday morning breakfast, or dessert, you'll find a tasty recipe that is sure to be enjoyed by people of all ages, especially the young at heart.

Καλή όρεξη

Mars Spanakopita

It's All Greek To Me

Antheia – an-thee-uh
Athena = a-**thee**-na
Aphrodite = aff-ro-**die**-tee
Atlas = at-**luh**-s
Ares = eh-r-**ee**-s
Artemis = are-**tem**-iss
Apollo = uh-**pol**-o
Boreas = **bo**-ree-as
Chronos =**cro**-nos
Demeter = dee-**meet**-er
Dionysus = **die**-on-eye-sus
Eirene = ee-**ree**-nee
Eros = **er**-os
Gaia = **guy**-uh
Hades = hay-**dees**
Helios = **hee**-lee-oss
Hera = **hair**-uh
Hestia = **hes**-t-uh
Heracles = **hair**-a-kleez
Hermes = **her**-meez
Iris = **eye**-ris
Kratos = **krat**-ohs
Mars= mars
Nike = ny-**kee**
Perseus = **per**-see-us
Pegasus = **peg**-a-sus
Poseidon = **poss**-eye-don
Proteus = **pro**-tee-us
Themis = **theem**-is
Triton = try-ton
Zeus = zoos

Athenian Frappe

Breakfast

Gaia Baklava Toast

SERVES: 4

Ingredients

3 eggs
1 cup milk
2 tablespoons cinnamon
4 tablespoons honey
4 slices of sliced thick bread
1 cup walnuts, finely chopped
1 tablespoon cinnamon
¼ teaspoon ground cloves
1 tablespoon sugar
1 banana, sliced

Method

1. In a bowl, beat eggs, milk, and cinnamon.
2. In another bowl, mix chopped walnuts, cinnamon, sugar, and ground cloves.
3. Spray large skillet with nonstick spray and heat to medium high.
4. Taking one slice of bread at a time, dip each piece of bread in the egg mixture and place it on the heated skillet.
5. Cook on each side for 3 to 4 minutes until golden brown. Pour honey over French toast and sprinkle the walnut mixture, sliced banana & drizzle with more honey.

Protein Pancakes and Waffles

- Make with your favorite protein waffle or pancake mix according to directions. Sprinkle with honey and walnut mixture.
- Take 2 ounces Greek yogurt and mix with fig spread. Top your waffles or pancakes.

Each French Toast is dipped in honey around the crust and rolled in a blend of baklava mixture. These are fun to make with the whole family.

Perseus Parfait

SERVES: 4

Ingredients

4 cups Greek plain yogurt
¼ cup walnuts, chopped
1 teaspoon ground cinnamon
3 tablespoons honey
½ cup raspberries
½ cup blueberries
¼ cup strawberries
¼ cup honey

Method

1. In a bowl, mix walnuts, and cinnamon reserving ¼ cup mixture. Mix in yogurt to the walnut mixture, while adding honey until smooth consistency.
2. In a parfait glass add walnut yogurt mixture then layer fresh fruit of choice, yogurt mixture, fruit and then yogurt. Garnish with a sprinkle of the walnut mixture on top, drizzle with honey, a raspberry and a mint leaf.

Family style option

- Place honey walnut yogurt mixture in a large serving bowl and sprinkle walnut mixture on top. Drizzle with honey and fresh fruit around the edges.

Greeks are known for their rich, smooth yogurt, which is a healthy source of protein. In this recipe, the creamy yogurt is topped with ingredients such as fruit, walnuts, cinnamon, and honey. This is a great start to your morning.

Olympic Omelets

SERVES: 2

Ingredients

4 eggs, beaten
¼ cup milk
¼ cup spinach leaves, freshly chopped
½ cup Feta cheese, crumbled
1 tomato, diced
¼ red bell pepper, diced
Sea salt and pepper to taste
1 avocado, sliced

Eat like a Greek god with this delicious Mediterranean-style omelet. Olympic omelets area a colorful array of spinach, red peppers and feta.

Method

1. Whisk eggs and milk together. Add salt and pepper.
2. Spray a nonstick omelet pan with nonstick spray and heat to a medium-high temperature.
3. When the pan is hot, place half of egg mixture in pan.
4. Once the egg mixture begins to solidify, place half of the spinach, Feta, tomato, and red bell pepper portions on one side of the egg.
5. Fold half of egg mixture over ingredients.
6. Cover with a steam lid that has a few drops of water inside it and cook until omelet is fully cooked and fluffy.
7. Repeat process to create the second omelet.
8. Sprinkle with dried chives and diced red bell peppers. Sprinkle with crumbled Feta. Serve with sliced avocado and toasted bread.

Hercules Protein Smoothie

SERVES: 2

Ingredients

1 cup plain Greek yogurt
½ cup pineapple juice
2 cups frozen pineapple chunks
¼ cup cream of coconut
1 cup ice cubes (optional)

Method

1. Combine yogurt, pineapple juice, frozen pineapple chunks, ice cubes, and cream of coconut, in a blender or bullet. Blend for 1–2 minutes until smooth.
2. Divide into two chilled glasses. Garnish with coconut whipped cream & toasted coconut shavings.

Hercules Light Protein Smoothie

1 cup frozen pineapple
1 cup Bai brand coconut drink

- Using blender or bullet, blend for 1–2 minutes until smooth mixture.

Power packed protein made with the perfect amount of pineapple and coconut will start your morning off the right. A delicious addition to your breakfast routine.

Athena's Cinnamon Honey Muffins

SERVES: 4

The Greek god,

Athena, means

wisdom. For breakfast,

these delicious

cinnamon muffins

are a wise choice.

Ingredients

1 cup plain authentic Greek yogurt
1 cup flour
2 teaspoons baking powder
1 teaspoon baking soda
½ teaspoon ground clove
4 Tablespoons ground cinnamon
1 cup granulated sugar
1 large egg
4 Tablespoons melted butter
2 teaspoons vanilla extract
½ cup milk
1 ½ chopped walnuts

Method

1. With a mixer, cream butter and sugar. Add egg and vanilla extract until well blended then add yogurt and milk.
2. In a separate bowl, combine flour, baking powder, baking soda, cinnamon and clove, and chopped walnuts.
3. Slowly add dry ingredients into the wet ingredients until evenly combined.
4. Spoon into muffin tin lined with paper muffin cases.
5. Bake in a preheated oven at 350ºF for 12–15 minutes until golden and firm. Cool slightly and lightly. Drizzle with honey & sprinkle with walnuts on top. As an optional topping, use coconut whipped cream.

Athenian Frappe

SERVES: 2

Frappe is a coffee enjoyed all day long. This frothy, instant coffee drink will be your new favorite drink for breakfast or anytime of the day. In Greece, there are three ways to make your frappe coffee: sketo, metrio or glyko.

Ingredients

1 ½ tablespoon Nescafe instant Greek coffee
1 ½ cups cold water
1 cup of ice cubes
1–2 teaspoons granulated sugar
¼ cup milk

Method

1. In a shaker, add coffee, 2 ounces of water and sugar to taste. With lid on shake for 30 seconds or electric drink mixer until you have a frothy foam.
2. In a tall glass, pour a frothy coffee mixture into the glass. It should be about half full. Add ice cubes into the glass & pour remaining water almost to the top leaving room for milk.
3. Add milk, "me gala" if desired.
4. Serve with a straw.

Frappe 3 different ways.

- **Sketo** Frappe (Plain) Only add instant coffee & water in the shaker with out sugar.
- **Metrio** Frappe (Medium) Add instant coffee, 1–2 teaspoons sugar & water to the shaker.
- **Glyko** Frappe (Sweet) Add instant coffee, 2–3 teaspoons sugar & water to the shaker.
- You can also add milk ***"me gala"*** if you want it with milk. A common order is **"ena frappe metrio me gala"** (a frappe with medium sugar and some milk).

Demeter Greek Salad

Soups and Salads

Hera Lentil Soup

SERVES: 4

Ingredients

1 pound dry green lentils
1 medium onion, chopped
2–3 cloves garlic, minced
1 stalk celery, d iced
1 medium carrot, diced
⅓ cup olive oil
2 teaspoons salt
3 bay leaves
1 Tablespoon red wine vinegar
6 cups water
1⅓ cups tomato sauce
Salt & pepper to taste

Method

1. Wash the lentils and soak in a bowl of warm water for 3–4 hours; change warm water every hour. Finally drain.
2. Add lentils to a pot and cover with an inch of water. Bring water and lentils to a boil. Boil for 15 minutes. Drain & rinse lentils.
3. Finely dice carrots, onions, celery, and garlic.
4. In a pot on medium heat, add olive oil and then the onions for about 5 minutes. Add carrots, celery, garlic and bay leaves. Cook for a few minutes constantly stirring. Then add lentils, tomato sauce, salt, pepper and water.
5. Bring to a boil for a few minutes, then reduce heat to medium. Cover with a lid and cook for 30 minutes. Lentils are done when they are soft. Add a splash of red wine vinegar to each serving. Serve with toasted banquette.

Lentils are found all over the Mediterranean, and are not only delicious, but healthy. Enjoy making this vegetarian lentil soup as a meal or as a starter to an entrée.

Artemis Egg Lemon Soup (Avgolemono)

SERVES: 4

Ingredients

3 eggs, separated
6 cups chicken broth
2 fresh lemon juice
1 cup rice
1 teaspoon sea salt and pepper

Method

1. Bring chicken broth to a boil. Add rice, salt and pepper to boiling broth; cook for 20 minutes or until tender. When rice is cooked, lower heat to simmer.
2. In a mixing bowl put 3 egg whites and beat until stiff. Then add the yolks continuing to whisk and beat well while adding the lemon juice. Then add the broth to egg, a thin stream a little at a time, beating well until most of the broth is used.
3. Pour mixture back into pot and stir vigorously over very low heat until it thickens. Do not boil or it will curdle.

Avgolemono (egg-lemon) soup is perhaps the most iconic of all Greek soups. Bursting with lemon flavor this soup is known as a natural healing elixir.

Demeter Greek Salad

SERVES 4

The Greek gods' knew the importance of a fresh salad. An array of garden vegetables that blend well with premium Greek olive oil and oregano. Adding feta at the end gives it a rich taste.

Ingredients

4 tomatoes, quartered
2 large cucumbers, sliced
1 quarter of a red onion, sliced
¼ cup Kalamata olives, pitted
4 ounces Feta cheese, in small cubes or crumbled
1 red pepper, sliced
1 green pepper, sliced
2 tablespoons capers
Sea salt and pepper to taste

Greek God's Salad Dressing

¾ cup Greek extra virgin olive oil
1 tablespoon oregano
1 teaspoon fresh lemon juice
Sea salt and black ground pepper to taste

Method

1. Prepare the dressing by whisking together the olive oil, salt, pepper, lemon and oregano. Set aside.
2. Cut the Feta cheese into 1-inch cubes and place in a salad bowl. Add tomatoes, cucumbers, capers, red and green peppers. Toss gently together.
3. Whisk the dressing well and pour over cucumber, Feta, and tomatoes. Sprinkle Kalamata olives over the top. Dust with a few sprinkles of oregano, salt, pepper and capers before serving.

Greek Green Goddess Dressing

SERVES: 4

Greek Green Goddess dressing is light and refreshing with a burst of flavor to the taste. Use as a dressing, dip or sandwich spread. Make this a vegan dressing by replacing Greek yogurt with avocado.

Ingredients

2 cups Greek authentic yogurt (Vegan alternative use 5 ounces avocado, mashed)
1 small lemon, juice strained
1½ Tablespoons fresh dill, chopped
1½ Tablespoons fresh chives chopped
2½ Tablespoons pesto, store bought
1 clove fresh garlic, minced
3 Tablespoons Greek extra virgin olive oil
½ cup water
Sea salt & pepper to taste

Method

1. Finely chop fresh dill, chives & garlic, set aside.
2. In the food processor, add yogurt, lemon juice, salt, pepper, dill, chives, garlic, pesto, olive oil & water.
3. Blend ingredients well in food processor for 3 minutes until dressing becomes a light green color & fully blended.
4. Drizzle over your favorite Greek salad or use as a dip.

Vegan Greek Green Goddess

- Replace Greek yogurt with 5 ounces of fresh avocados and continue to follow above recipe.

Aria Garden of the Gods Bowl

SERVES: 2

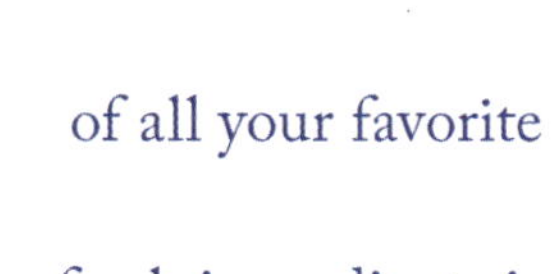

A full vegetarian meal of all your favorite fresh ingredients in a bowl. Great as a salad or as an entrée.

Ingredients

2 cups mixed greens
1 Tablespoon fresh lemon juice strained
1 Tablespoons fresh chives, chopped
½ cup hummus, favorite store bought
¼ cup Kalamata olives, pitted & sliced
1 seedless cucumber, sliced
1 cup quinoa
1 tablespoon oregano
1 slice pita or naan bread, sliced
1 red bell pepper, sliced
½ cup crumbled Feta cheese—optional
Sea salt & pepper to taste
¼ cup extra virgin olive oil

Method

1. Chop chives, cucumbers, bell pepper and slice Kalamata olives.
2. Cook quinoa according to instructions and set aside.
3. In a large bowl, place mixed greens. In the middle a large dollop of hummus. Around the edges of the bowl in sections, place red bell pepper, kalamata olives, cucumbers, feta cheese, quinoa, and sliced feta or naan bread. Sprinkle oregano and chopped chives over ingredients. Drizzle with olive oil & lemon juice or Greek Green Goddess dressing. See recipe in cookbook.

Chronos Watermelon Berry Salad

SERVES: 4

Ingredients

4 watermelon slices, cut ½ inch thick
½ red onion, sliced
¼ cup Kalamata olives
4 ounces Feta, sliced in a cube or crumbled
1 cup baby arugula lettuce
½ cup blueberries
½ cup raspberries
½ cup Greek extra virgin olive oil
Sea salt and pepper to taste
1 tablespoon balsamic glaze
¼ cup fresh pomegranates
¼ cup honey

This recipe is great for summer. A blend of watermelon, berries, and Feta cheese makes this a refreshing and tantalizing part of any meal. Great on toasted Tuscan bread.

Method

1. Taking a star shaped cookie cutter, cut 8 stars from watermelon or simply slice into cubes. Place arugula, sliced onions, watermelon in a large serving bowl and top with berries.
2. Drizzle olive oil over ingredients. Sprinkle with salt, pepper and oregano.
3. Garnish with feta, olives and pomegranates on top of the salad. Drizzle with balsamic glaze and honey.

Tuscan Bread Salad Option

- Cut a loaf Tuscan or Ciabatta bread in half horizontally. In a 400-degree oven, toast for 10 minutes. Spread your favorite soft goat cheese on toasted bread. Dust with salt, pepper & oregano. Top with arugula, olive oil, watermelon and follow recipe above.

Themis Tzatziki

Appetizers

Triton Dill Tiropitas

Flaky filo layers folded into triangles and stuffed with a blend of feta cheese. These make a delicious appetizer anytime of the day. For an extra sweetness, drizzle with honey.

SERVES: 4

Ingredients

1 cup Feta cheese, crumbled
1 ½ cups small curd cottage cheese
2 eggs, beaten
1 stick butter, melted
1 package filo, thawed
1 Tablespoon fresh dill, chopped

Method

1. In a large bowl, beat two eggs well and mix in the Feta and cottage cheese. Mixwell. Melt butter and set aside.
2. Keeping filo in a long roll, cut into three equal parts. Unroll the first portion and cover with a cloth to prevent from drying out.
3. Place parchment paper on a work service, take one sheet of filo on your work surface. Using a pastry brush. Butter filo and take another sheet of filo one on top of the other. Lightly butter second sheet.
4. Take one teaspoon of the Feta cheese mixture and place it in the bottom right hand corner of the filo sheet. Starting from the corner with filling, fold the dough in triangles using a flag-folding technique. Tuck and fold making a triangle.
5. Lightly seal with the butter.
6. Place each completed tiropita on a parchment lined cookie sheet, seal side down. Repeat the process with the remaining filling and filo. Bake at 350° F for 25 to 30 minutes or until golden brown.

Optional

- add 1 tablespoon chopped Kalamata olives to cheese blend.

Mars Spanakopita

SERVES: 6

Ingredients

- 10 ounces fresh spinach, chopped
- 1 bunch of green onions, chopped
- 1 small yellow onion, chopped
- ½ cup Greek extra virgin olive oil
- 2–3 tablespoons fresh or dried dill
- 10 ounces Feta cheese, crumbled
- 1 cup small curd cottage cheese
- 2 eggs, beaten
- 1 pound filo, thawed
- 2 sticks of butter, melted
- Sea salt and pepper

Method

1. Sauté onions in a pan with 4 tablespoons of olive oil.
2. In a bowl, mix sautéed onions with spinach, Feta, eggs, dill, salt, pepper, and remaining olive oil.
3. Unwrap filo and lay flat covering with a cloth. On a parchment lined work service, place one filo sheet. Using a pastry brush, lightly brush filo with melted butter. Place another filo sheet on top of the first filo sheet and lightly butter.
4. Take ½ cup of the spinach mixture and place in the middle edge of the filo's short end.
5. Fold edges in overlapping and continue to roll filo keeping a rectangle shape until finished.
6. Lightly butter seal and place on a parchment lined baking sheet. Repeat the process until all are complete.
7. Bake at 350° F for 25 to 30 minutes until golden brown.

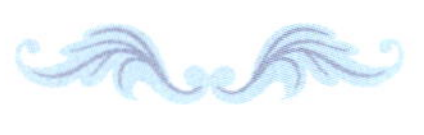

Spanakopita contains deliciously prepared spinach and Feta cheese wrapped in layers of filo dough pouches. A Greek favorite that can be served as an appetizer or a vegetarian meal.

Antheia Cheese Kisses

These simple, bite-sized appetizers are full of sweet and savory flavor. The perfect appetizer as an addition to your charcutier board.

SERVES: 4

Pistachio Kisses Mixture—Ingredients

½ cup pistachios, finely chopped
6 ounces creamy chevre (goat cheese)
6 sundried tomatoes or kalamata olive, sliced

Baklava Kisses Mixture—Ingredients

1 cup walnuts, finely chopped
¼ cup walnuts, chopped
1 teaspoon ground cinnamon
¼ teaspoon ground clove
2–3 Tablespoons honey

Method—Pistachio Kisses

1. Scoop a heaping ½ teaspoon of goat cheese and press a sundried tomato or Kalamata olive into the center.
2. Wrap cheese around sundried tomato or Kalamata olive to form a ball. Repeat to finish making balls.
3. Place nuts in a small bowl. Roll the ball into the chopped nuts to create a crust; set each on a plate. Repeat with remaining ingredients until finished. Refrigerate until ready to serve.
4. The kisses will keep for up to three days if stored covered in the refrigerator. Place a fancy toothpick in the center of each to serve.

Method—Baklava Kisses

1. In a bowl, mix walnuts, cinnamon, sugar and clove. Split mixture in two separate bowls.
2. Scoop ½ tablespoon of goat cheese and press 1 teaspoon of baklava mixture into the center while rolling & mixing into a ball. Repeat steps above to finish making balls.
3. Roll the balls into walnut mixture to create a crust; set each on a plate and drizzle with honey. Refrigerate until ready to serve.

Boreas Baked Feta Cheese

SERVES: 4

Baked feta topped with fresh ingredients melts to perfection with a fusion of flavors. Wrap in filo dough and bake as an elegant appetizer option.

Ingredients

7 ounces whole Feta cheese
1 Tablespoon dry oregano
¼ cup red onion, thinly sliced
1 tomato, diced
2 Tablespoons capers
¼ cup Kalamata olives, pitted & sliced
1 clove garlic, minced
2 Tablespoons Greek extra virgin olive oil
1 teaspoon black pepper

Method

1. Preheat oven to 350 degrees. Cut large sheet of aluminum foil. Take feta out of the brine & slice through the middle. Place each feta cheese square in center of aluminum foil.
2. On top of feta cheese sprinkle with oregano, tomatoes, red onions, capers, olives, salt and pepper. Drizzle the top with olive oil and seal foil around the cheese. Place on baking sheet and bake for 15 minutes.
3. Carefully open packets. Transfer the feta cheese to a plate and serve with baguette slices or pita.

Filo Baked Pouches

- Take a piece of thawed filo dough, using melted butter brush the entire sheet. Repeat with another filo sheet. Place plain feta square in the middle of one end of filo, fold edges in over lapping and continue folding filo to neatly wrapped package of feta. Bake at 350 degrees for 15 minutes or until filo is browned. Top with drizzled honey and sprinkle with black & white sesame seeds. Serve warm with bread.

Dionysius Stuffed Grape Leaves (Dolmathes)

SERVES: 6

Ingredients

2 pounds lean hamburger
3 tablespoons fresh mint, chopped
1 cup white rice
1 large yellow onion, finely chopped
1 cup water
2 tablespoons olive oil
19 grape leaves from the jar (found in specialty food or online)
1 large fresh lemon, sliced
5 whole celery stalks, cut in half
Sea salt and pepper

The god Dionysius is known for grapes and abundance. Dionysius grape leaves are stuffed with ground beef and rice with a hint of fresh mint.

Method

1. In a bowl, mix hamburger, dried mint, rice, onion, salt, and pepper.
2. Flatten each grape leaf and snip off any excess stems with scissors.
3. Take a leaf and place it vein side up. Place a tablespoon of meat mixture in the shape of a small cigar at the base of the stem. Roll it once and then tuck in sides and continue to roll tightly. Repeat until all are complete.
4. Place celery first and then each rolled grape leaf on the bottom of a deep pot, leaving no gaps. Pour 1 cup of water and 2 tablespoons olive oil along with half the juice of one lemon. Place a small plate over the top of the tightly packed grape leaves to keep them from boiling over. On medium heat, slowly simmer for 1 hour until the leaves are tender.
5. Discarding celery, place grape leaves on platter & serve with lemon wedge or tzatziki (see recipe in cookbook).

Vegetarian Option

- Leave out the ground beef and double the rice to 2 cups.

Ares Fire Red Pepper Dip

A spicy feta dip is made with roasted red peppers, feta and fresh herbs. Add red pepper flakes to give a little kick of heat to your dip.

SERVES: 4

Ingredients

8 ounces feta cheese
12 ounce jar roasted red peppers, drained
¼ cup roasted garlic
2 teaspoons fresh squeezed lemon juice
¼ cup extra virgin olive oil
1 tablespoon chopped fresh oregano
Sea salt and pepper taste
½ teaspoon red pepper flakes (optional)

Method

1. Place all ingredients in a food processor or blender slowly adding olive oil.
2. Slowly adding olive oil to make smooth mixture.
3. Season to taste with sea salt and pepper.
4. To add added heat to dip, add red pepper flakes.
5. Serve with baguette, sliced pita bread or vegetables.

Themis Tzatziki

SERVES: 4–6

Ingredients

1 cup Greek plain yogurt
1 seedless English cucumber, grated with skin
2 tablespoons dry dill weed (optional)
¼ cup fresh mint, chopped (optional)
2 garlic cloves, minced
1 tablespoon fresh lemon juice
1 tablespoons Greek extra virgin olive oil.
½ teaspoon sea salt & pepper to taste

Method

1. Using a cheese grater, grate the entire cucumber using large holes.
2. Tightly squeeze the cucumber of any excess liquid. Discard excess juice.
3. Fold the cucumber into the yogurt. Add mint, dill, garlic, lemon juice, salt, pepper and olive oil remaining ingredients in a bowl.
4. Place in a decorative bowl. Drizzle with olive oil and place a Kalamata olive in the center.
5. Serve with sliced pita bread wedges either grilled or heated.

Vegan Tzatziki

- Replace Greek yogurt with 1 cup mashed avocado and continue with above recipe.

This dip is full of fresh herbs, cucumbers and Greek yogurt. Tzatziki's refreshing cucumber flavor will add zip to any appetizer, sandwich or meal. Serve with vegetables or pita bread.

Aphrodite's Antipasto Kebabs

SERVES: 4

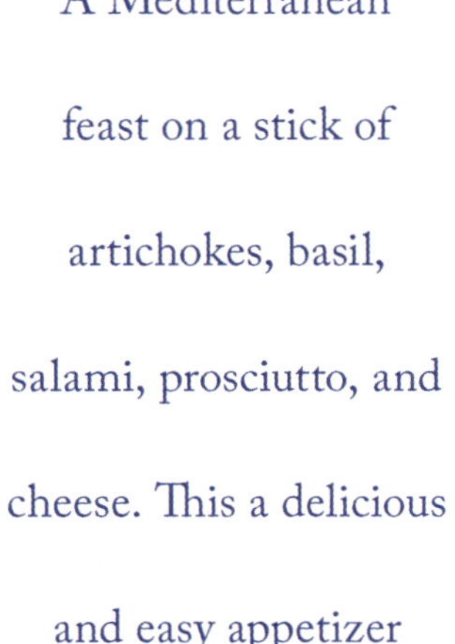

A Mediterranean feast on a stick of artichokes, basil, salami, prosciutto, and cheese. This a delicious and easy appetizer or side to an entrée.

Ingredients

- ½ cup Greek extra virgin olive oil
- ¼ cup red wine vinegar
- 1 teaspoon lemon peel, grated
- 1 clove garlic, sliced
- 1 teaspoon oregano
- ½ pound buffalo mozzarella small balls or cubed feta
- 4 prosciutto slices
- 8 slices hard salami, cut in half slices
- ½ cup Kalamata pitted olives
- 10 basil leaves
- 7 ounces marinated quartered artichokes, drained
- 20 cheese tortellini, fully cooked
- Sea salt & pepper to taste.
- 20 bamboo skewers (4-inch) or rosemary sprigs

Method

1. In a medium bowl, mix olive oil, vinegar, lemon peel, garlic, and oregano to make marinade.
2. In boiling water, add your favorite tortellini. Boil until cooked. Drain & set aside.
3. Cut prosciutto slices lengthwise into 1-inch strips.
4. Pleat fold prosciutto pieces and spear prosciutto, mozzarella, basil, salami with skewers; add assortment of olives, artichokes, tortellini and cheese of choice to skewers.
5. On plate, brush antipasto skewers with marinade. Dust with salt, pepper & oregano.

Helios Tzatziki Pizza

SERVES: 4–6

Ingredients

1 12-inch flatbread pizza crust, store bought
½ pounds mozzarella cheese, shredded
1 (8 ounce can) marinated artichokes, sliced
½ cup Kalamata olives, pitted
2 Roma tomatoes, diced
1 red pepper, thinly sliced
½ cup fresh spinach leaves, chopped
1 teaspoon oregano
2 green onions, chopped
4 ounces Feta cheese, crumbled
¼ cup fresh basil, chopped
Sea salt and black pepper to taste
2 cups Tzatziki—See recipe in cookbook.

Method

1. Spread tzatziki over the flatbread or pizza crust, covering entirely.
2. Layer with artichokes, tomatoes, red peppers, spinach, green onions, and olives. Sprinkle with crumbled Feta, mozzarella cheese, basil and dust with oregano, salt, and pepper.
3. Bake at 350° F for 15 to 20 minutes or until cheese is melted. Slice into wedges and serve. After baking, dollop with tzatziki over the top of cooked flatbread.

Helios Greek pizza is fully loaded with Mediterranean flavor and fresh herbs. The secret sauce is the tzatziki.

Apollo Filo Artichoke Dip

SERVES: 6

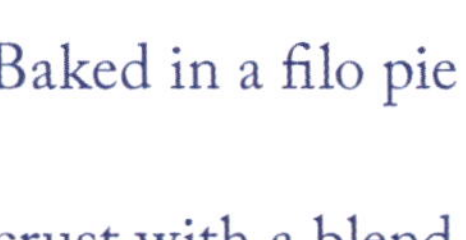

Baked in a filo pie crust with a blend of artichokes, feta cheese and herbs. This elegant appetizer will impress your guests.

Ingredients

- 10 quartered marinated artichokes, drained and chopped
- 8 ounces cream cheese, softened
- ½ cup cottage cheese
- 2 cups feta cheese, crumbled
- ½ cup Parmesan cheese
- 2 eggs, beaten
- 2 tablespoons dry dill
- 8 teaspoons butter, melted
- 1 teaspoon sea salt
- 1 teaspoon pepper
- 1 filo dough, thawed
- 2 tablespoons extra virgin Greek olive oil

Method

1. Preheat oven to 360 degrees Fahrenheit. Lightly butter a 13×9 glass pie dish and set aside.
2. In a large bowl, combine softened cream cheese, cottage cheese, feta, and olive oil. Mix well adding eggs, dill, Parmesan cheese, salt and pepper.
3. Take filo package and carefully unroll flat. Cover unused sheets. Using pastry brush, laying 4 sheets out, butter each one & lay on the bottom to cover dish to cover. Tuck in filo edges
4. Spoon artichoke mixture into the pie dish and smooth the top to make level.
5. To make filo crust, start by laying the filo horizontal. Butter one sheet of filo at a time and gather like a fan style approx. 1 inch high. Starting at pie pan outer edge, place filo fan around the edges picking off where one ended

and starting another. Continue buttering filo fans and placing in the pie dish continuing where filo finished in a serpentine manner. The entire top will create a filo flower.

6. Bake at 360 degrees Fahrenheit for 20-25 minutes until lightly browned on top. Serve warm with crackers or baguette.

Triton Shrimp Santorini

Entrees

Proteus Kalamata Olive Shrimp Pasta

SERVES: 4

A light and refreshing dill dressing served over shrimp, tomatoes, olives, and orzo pasta. Great for a picnic or family gathering.

Salad Ingredients

1 pound large shrimp, cooked, peeled, and deveined
1 cup orzo or farfalle pasta, cooked
4 ounces Feta cheese, crumbled
1 large Roma tomato, diced
15 Kalamata olives, pitted and sliced
2 green onions, chopped

Dressing Ingredients

1 teaspoon fresh or dried dill
1½ teaspoons garlic cloves, minced
3 tablespoons Greek extra virgin olive oil
1 tablespoon fresh squeezed lemon juice
1 teaspoon red wine vinegar
½ teaspoon sea salt and black pepper to taste

Method

1. Boil orzo pasta until fully cooked. Rinse and toss with 1 tablespoon olive oil. Mix pasta with shrimp, tomato, chopped olives, and onions.
2. Using a separate bowl to make dressing, combine oil, lemon juice, vinegar, salt, dill, and garlic. Whisk well and add pepper to taste. Pour over shrimp orzo pasta.
3. Sprinkle top with crumbled Feta cheese, salt & pepper. Cover and refrigerate.

Zeus Sliders

SERVES: 4

Ingredients

1 pound lean ground beef or ground lamb
2 tablespoons plain bread crumbs
1 tablespoon lemon juice
2 teaspoons dried oregano
1 teaspoon mint, finely chopped
½ teaspoon salt
1–2 cloves of garlic, chopped
6 mini pita breads or mini buns
2 tomatoes, sliced
½ cucumber, julienned
¼ red onion, thinly sliced
½ cup tzatziki topping (see tzatziki recipe in cookbook)

Method

1. In a large bowl, mix hamburger, bread crumbs, lemon juice, oregano, mint, garlic, and salt.
2. Shape beef mixture into patties about ¼ inch thick.
3. Cook patties medium heat on nonstick grill or grill. Cook one side for 3 minutes and flip patties to cook for 3 more minutes until inside temperature is 160°F. Add feta cheese while cooking the second side. Remove patties.
4. Place patties on toasted bun bottom or pita. Top with slices of tomato, cucumber, red onion, feta and top with tzatziki sauce Serve open face.

The Zeus burger is made with Mediterranean spices and will add variety to an everyday burger. Serve open face topped with melted Feta cheese,

Ares Spanapasta

SERVES: 4

A perfect blend of spinach, feta, lemon & dill sauce tossed in pasta. Adding egg to the mixture makes a delicious creamy sauce.

Ingredients

- 16 ounces chopped spinach
- 5 green onions, chopped
- ½ cup Greek extra virgin olive oil
- 3 tablespoons fresh or dried dill
- 6 ounces Feta cheese, crumbled
- 1 lemon, strained juice–1 teaspoon grated lemon zest
- 6 ounces of spaghetti or barilla protein spaghetti
- 2 eggs (optional)
- 2 tablespoons Sea salt and black cracked pepper

Method

1. Boil water in a pan with a teaspoon of salt. To boiling water, add pasta cook until al dente. Reserve 1½ cups pasta water, then drain pasta.
2. In a bowl, add Feta, dill, black pepper, lemon zest, lemon juice and optional 2 eggs. Whisk well.
3. Sauté onions in a large pan with 4 tablespoons olive oil on medium heat for 1–2 minutes until softened. Add spinach in pan with 1 tablespoon dill, salt and pepper. Sauté until fully cooked.
4. Add pasta into the pan with spinach & onions. Lightly mix so the spinach mixture is blended well with the pasta.
5. Add into the pasta, feta, lemon, egg mixture as well half of reserved pasta water. Stirring everything together until fully cooked. Let the pasta finish cooking in the sauce for a few minutes. If the pasta seems dry add a little more pasta water. Top with extra feta, olive oil & lemon juice.

Triton Shrimp Santorini

SERVES: 4

Ingredients

¼ cup Greek extra virgin olive oil
5 green onions, chopped
½ medium yellow onion, chopped
1–2 garlic clove, minced
1 ½ pounds large uncooked shrimp, shelled and deveined
5 Roma tomatoes, sliced thin wedges
¼ cup dry white wine
4 ounces Feta cheese, cubed or crumbled
2 tablespoons dried dill
¼ teaspoon salt
¼ teaspoon black pepper
1 cup orzo pasta, cooked

Method

1. Clean shrimp. Rinse and dry with paper towels. Set aside.
2. On medium heat in a sauce pan, gently sauté onions and garlic in olive oil until softened.
3. Turn heat to medium -high. Add tomatoes, dill, wine, salt, and freshly ground black pepper. Continue to stir and simmer for 10 minutes. Add shrimp to tomato sauce & lower heat to medium-low. Cover with a lid and simmer for 20–25 minutes until tomatoes are reduced.
4. In pan of boiling water, add salt and cook orzo pasta according to directions.
5. Pour drained orzo pasta in a baking dish then tomato sauce. Mix thoroughly and top with Feta cheese.
6. In oven with broiler on high, bake for 5 minutes until feta cheese is softened then serve.

This recipe was inspired by the sea and the island of Santorini where one can eat fruit of the sea daily. May this entree bring you closer to the Greek Islands.

Nike Chicken Gyros

SERVES 4

Pronounced "yee-ros," which translates to round. This pita bread sandwich is stacked high with marinated meat, tomatoes, onions, and the secret special sauce. For a healthier version, make Gyro lettuce wraps.

Ingredients

4 (4 ounce) chicken breasts
3 tomatoes, sliced
¼ cup red onion, chopped
1 cup tzatziki topping sauce (recipe in cookbook)
4 pieces pita bread, heated or grilled

Greek Oregano Lemon Marinade

¾ cup Greek extra virgin olive oil
2 tablespoon oregano
2 tablespoons lemon juice
Sea salt and pepper to taste

Method

1. In a bowl, make marinade by whisking olive oil, oregano, lemon juice, salt, and pepper. Place meat in marinade and mix well.
2. Prepare tzatziki topping sauce. See recipe in cookbook.
3. Dice tomatoes and chopped onions. Set aside.
4. Cook marinated chicken on outdoor grill or nonstick grill pan on medium heat until fully cooked until the inside temperature is 160° F. Slice into strips and set aside.
5. Brush pita bread with olive oil and lightly brown on a grill or warm in an oven.
6. Take each piece of heated or grilled pita bread, top with some grilled chicken or steak, tomatoes, and onions, and then add a dollop of tzatziki topping sauce.

Gyro Lettuce Wrap Option

- Replace the pita bread with a large romaine lettuce leaf.
- Follow above cooking directions. Place chicken, tomato, lettuce, onions, and tzatziki sauce in romaine lettuce leaf.

Hermes Pasta

SERVES 4

A Greek-style sauce with a hint of cinnamon served over pasta. Top with béchamel sauce for a deconstructed Pastitsio.

Ingredients

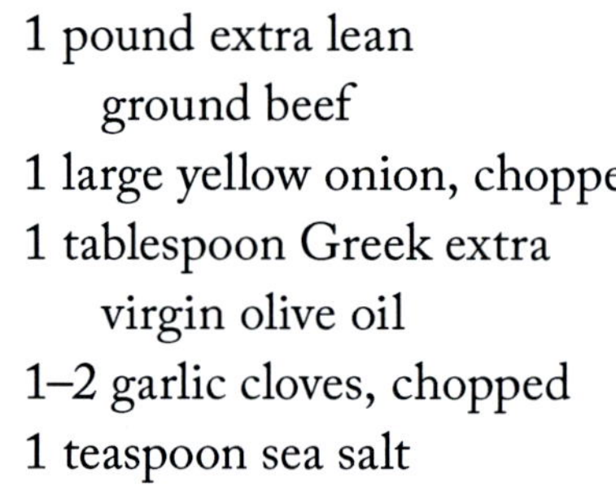

- 1 pound extra lean ground beef
- 1 large yellow onion, chopped
- 1 tablespoon Greek extra virgin olive oil
- 1–2 garlic cloves, chopped
- 1 teaspoon sea salt
- 1 teaspoon black pepper
- 1 ½ tablespoons ground cinnamon
- 16 tablespoons butter
- 1 cup tomato sauce
- 1 pound bucatini, Misko No. 2 macaroni pasta or mostaccioli
- 2 ½ cups Parmesan grated cheese

Method

1. Boil pasta until al dente. Strain pasta and mix in 1 tablespoon butter. Set aside.
2. In a large skillet over medium-high heat, sauté chopped onions and garlic in ½ stick of butter. Place ground beef in pan until completely browned and crumbled.
3. Add cinnamon, salt, and pepper to taste then mix in tomato sauce. Turn heat to medium low and simmer for 30 minutes.
4. Place pasta in a large oval serving platter, mix well with parmesan cheese and melted butter. Top the middle with meat sauce with béchamel sauce (change to "meat sauce and drizzle with bechamel sauce) (continue with béchamel sauce recipe).

Bechamel Sauce Recipe

Ingredients

3 tablespoons butter
3 tablespoons flour
1 cup Parmesan cheese
3 cups milk
1 tablespoon cinnamon

Method

1. In a deep saucepan on medium-high heat, melt 3 tablespoons butter slowly while whisking in 3 tablespoons of flour, little by little. Stir constantly until a thick paste forms. Add more flour as needed.
2. Slowly add warmed milk whisking until the liquid thickens. Constantly stirring, add another cup until the liquid thickens again, making sure to work out lumps and a smooth consistency. Once the sauce is thickened, add 2 cups Parmesan cheese and stir.
3. Place Hermes Pasta on a large oval serving platter topped with cinnamon meat sauce keeping a pasta border. Then béchamel over middle of the prepared pasta sauce. Sprinkle with additional Parmesan Cheese and dust top with cinnamon.

Pastitsio is a traditional Greek lasagna

Hermes Deconstructed Pastitsio

1. "Prepare Hermes Pasta recipe according to directions.
2. Place prepared parmesan, butter pasta in an oven safe dish, then top with a layer of Hermes meat pasta sauce. Finally, in the middle of meat sauce add a layer of Bechamel.
3. Sprinkle top of Bechamel with parmesan cheese & cinnamon.
4. Place in a 350 degree oven for 30-35 minutes.

Poseidon Filo Wrapped Baklava Salmon

SERVES: 4

Unique and flavorful is the best way to describe this tasty entrée. A delicious combination of sweet and savory flavors deliciously baked on salmon.

Ingredients

1 whole skinless salmon (1.5–2 pounds)
2 tablespoons honey
1½ cups walnuts, chopped
½ teaspoon cinnamon
¼ teaspoon ground clove
4 tablespoons butter, melted
2 sheets filo, thawed

Method

1. In a bowl, combine walnuts, cinnamon, and ground clove.
2. On a parchment sheet, place one filo sheet and butter with pastry brush. One on top of butter filo, repeat with second filo sheet and lightly butter. Place whole salmon in the middle of buttered filo.
3. Top entire salmon with prepared walnut mixture quickly before filo dries out. Starting at one end: gather & crinkle edges of filo around the salmon creating a border to encrust edges of salmon. Keep top of salmon exposed.
4. Gently, transfer salmon with parchment paper to baking sheet.
5. Bake in an oven at 360° F for 25 minutes or until salmon is fully cooked. Transfer to a serving platter and cut parchment edges. Drizzle entire salmon with honey and serve.

Baklava Salmon Option

- Omitting filo step, place whole salmon on parchment lined baking sheet and top with prepared walnut mixture. Continue to follow above baking instructions.

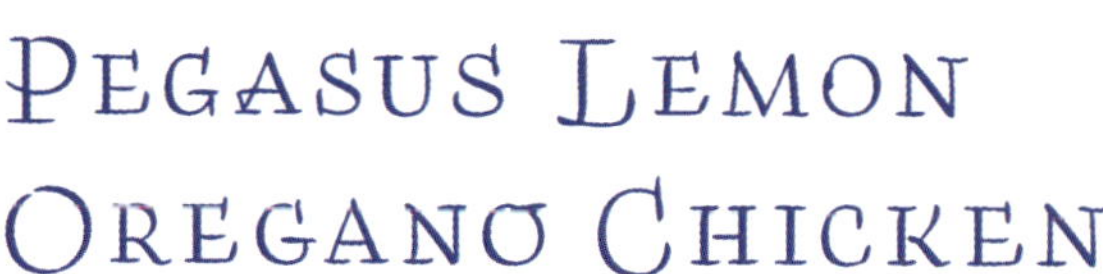

Pegasus Lemon Oregano Chicken

SERVES: 4

Pegasus lemon oregano chicken is best week night dinner. Marinated with a flavorful blend of lemon and oregano that is bursting with flavor.

Ingredients

4 chicken breasts, boneless
2–3 large fresh lemons, juice
3 tablespoons dried oregano
1 cup Greek extra virgin olive oil
5 potatoes, peeled and quartered
1 cup water
1 tablespoon black pepper
½ tablespoon Sea salt to taste

Method

1. In a baking dish, place quartered potatoes with chicken on top.
2. Make marinade by whisking olive oil, oregano, 1 lemon, salt, and pepper in a large bowl. Mix well and pour over chicken and potatoes. Toss to coat everything well.
3. Pour water in dish. Squeeze half a fresh lemon over everything in dish and sprinkle more oregano, salt, and pepper on top according to taste.
4. Cover and cook in oven at 360° Fahrenheit for 35 to 40 minutes, basting with marinade occasionally. Remove cover and squeeze more fresh lemon over the top of chicken. Cook another 15 to 20 minutes. Chicken should be fully cooked and golden brown. When chicken is fully cooked, take it out. Continue baking and basting the potatoes until golden brown.

Atlas Baklava

Sweets & Treats

Athenian Braided Cookies (Koulouria)

Koulouria dough is sweet and made with a hint of orange zest and vanilla. Fun to braid and create these cookies with the whole family.

MAKES 30–35

Dough Ingredients

- 1 cup butter, softened
- 1 cup sugar
- 3 eggs
- ¼ cup milk
- ½ teaspoon baking soda
- 3 teaspoons baking powder
- 3 teaspoons vanilla
- 5 cups flour
- 1 tablespoon orange zest

Topping Ingredients

- 1 egg, beaten
- 2 tablespoons sugar
- 2 tablespoons cinnamon

Method

1. With a mixer, blend butter and sugar together until light and fluffy for 3–4 minutes. Then beat in one egg at a time again until fluffy. Add milk, orange zest and vanilla while continuing to beat.
2. Mix only a few cups of flour with baking powder and soda. Add to the creamed mixture then slowly add the remaining mixed flour one cup at a time. With your hands, knead dough well. Use flour as needed. The dough should be easy to roll but not greasy or too dry, but a play dough-like consistency.
3. Take a tablespoon and roll a long, thin strip approximately 11 inches long. Then fold it by making a tall, even arch, Take each end over each other twisting to make a braid.

4. Brush with a beaten egg and leave plain or sprinkle with the cinnamon sugar mixture. Place on baking sheet and bake for 20 minutes at 350° F until golden brown. Serve with coffee. Great to dip into coffee.

Atlas Baklava Filo Triangles

Baklava is the most popular dessert of the Mediterranean. This baklava version is delicious and takes half the time to make. Layers of filo are folded into triangles and stuffed with walnut mixture.

MAKES 25-30

Baklava Ingredients

1 stick unsalted butter, melted
1 pound filo, thawed
2 pounds walnuts, chopped
2 tablespoons cinnamon
½ cup sugar
1 teaspoon ground cloves
50 whole cloves
50 baking cups

Syrup Ingredients

3 cups water
3 cups sugar
1 strip lemon zest and orange zest
1 pint of honey
½ fresh lemon, juiced and strained
1 cinnamon stick

Method

1. In a bowl, mix walnuts, cinnamon, sugar, and cloves. Set aside.
2. Keeping filo in a roll, cut into three equal parts. Unroll the first portion flat and cover with a cloth to prevent dryness. Place a filo sheet on the work surface and butter. Place a second filo sheet on top and lightly butter. One on top of the other.
3. Take one teaspoon of walnut mixture and in the bottom right hand corner of the filo sheets. Starting from the corner with the walnut filling, fold the dough into triangles using a flag-folding technique. Tucking and rolling to keep a tight triangle. Lightly brush the top edge with butter to seal it.

4. Place each completed triangle on cookie sheet. Place a clove in the center of triangle. Continue completing the remaining.
5. Bake at 360° F for 25 to 30 minutes or until golden brown. Drizzle with honey or continue on to make below syrup recipe.

To make the syrup

1. Boil water, sugar, lemon juice, cinnamon stick, orange zest and lemon zest for 20 minutes. Add one pint of honey, and then boil another 20 minutes, constantly scraping the foam off the top.
2. Reduce heat and remove zest and cinnamon stick. Slightly cool syrup.
3. Place cooled baklava triangles in a deep tin pan. Pour warm (not hot) syrup over cooled triangles. Soak for a few minutes.
4. Slightly drain and place each piece in a decorative baking cup and serve.

Eirene Powdered Sugar Cookies

MAKES: 50–60

Ingredients

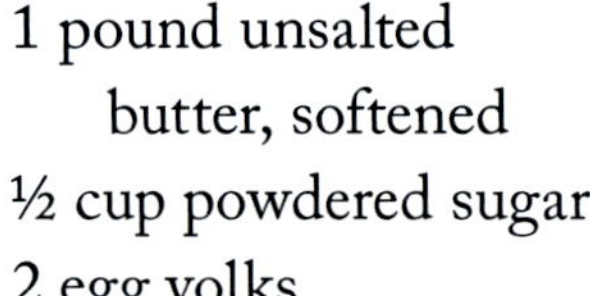

1 pound unsalted butter, softened
½ cup powdered sugar
2 egg yolks
1 teaspoon baking powder
3 tablespoons almond extract
4 cups of flour (may not need all)
6 cups of powdered sugar, sifted
60 baking cups

An easy-to-make, buttery cookie with powdered sugar. Known in Greece as Kourmabiethes. A cookie that celebrates events in life.

Method

1. In a mixer on medium high speed, cream butter and sugar until light and fluffy for 2–3minutes. Lower speed and add egg yolks one at a time, along with add almond extract.
2. In a separate bowl, mix flour and baking powder. Add flour little-by-little to buttered mixture . Continue to mix (preferably with hands) until dough is a little greasier than dry consistency. May need to add additional flour to get dough to feel like play dough.
3. Form a small, smooth ball and lightly pinch with three fingers on top. Place on a cookie sheet.
4. Bake in a preheated oven at 350° F for 20 to 25 minutes or until light brown in color. Let cool.
5. Line table with wax paper and lightly sift powdered sugar over paper. Place cookies on top of the powdered sugar. Continue to sift powdered sugar over cookies until they are completely covered with a mountain of sugar. Place in decorative baking cups.

Kratos Filo Cream Cheese Puffs

MAKES 10-15

A cream filled filo pastry that is baked to a golden brown and dusted with powdered sugar. Add a fun presentation flair to these filo dessert puffs by drizzling with chocolate or raspberry sauce.

Ingredients

1 package of filo, thawed
2 ounces cream cheese
1 tablespoon vanilla
2 egg yolks
1½ cup powdered sugar
2 sticks butter, melted

Method

1. In a bowl, mix softened cream cheese, vanilla, egg yolks and ½ cup powdered sugar.
2. Take unwrapped filo log and cut in half. Take one half of roll & lay flat coving with a clean dish towel. Take one filo sheet using a pastry brush filo lightly with butter. Repeat with a second sheet on top of the first.
3. Take ½ cup of cream cheese mixture and place in the middle of the filo's vertical or shortest end.
4. Fold edges in and roll the filo, keeping a flat, tight small rectangle.
5. Lightly butter the edges to seal the roll.
6. Place on a parchment lined cookie sheet, seam down. Repeat the process for each roll.
7. Bake at 350° F for 25 to 30 minutes on a cookie sheet until golden brown. With remaining sift powdered sugar over tops of cooled cream cheese puffs.
8. Drizzle with raspberry or chocolate sauce along with fresh raspberries.

Eros Loukoumathes Honey Donuts

Greek donuts, known as loukoumathes, are light, fluffy, and stacked high with honey, cinnamon, and nuts. These donots are great served with vanilla ice cream. Legend tells that this recipe was offered as a winner's reward during the first Olympic games.

MAKES: 10–15

Batter Ingredients

- 1 package active dry yeast
- ¼ cup water
- 1 cup milk, lukewarm
- 1 tablespoon & 1 teaspoon sugar
- 1 egg, beaten
- ¼ cup butter, melted
- 2 cups all-purpose flour
- ½ teaspoon salt
- Vegetable Oil (for frying)

Topping Ingredients

- 1 pint honey, warm
- 5 tablespoons ground cinnamon
- ½ cup walnuts, finely chopped (optional)

Method

1. Dissolve yeast in a large measuring cup with ¼ cup 120-degree water and a teaspoon of sugar to activate. Mix and cover with a plate. Place under a light until it doubles in size.
2. In a separate bowl, add milk, 1 tablespoon sugar, egg, and lukewarm melted butter. Then add activated yeast.
3. Sift flour and salt into a warm bowl and gradually stir in mixed liquids. Beat until smooth and continue beating for 1 minute.
4. Cover with a folded cloth and leave in a warm place for 1 ½ hours. Batter should double in bulk and have bubbles on the surface.
5. In a large pot or fryer, heat oil to 350° F.

6. Stir batter well. Take a teaspoon of dough, use a small spoon to push dough ball off, into deep hot oil. (Drop 4 or 5 balls at a time.) They should float to the top right away. Turn to brown evenly. Takes about 1 minute to cook. Remove with slotted spoon.
7. Drain on a paper towel. Place loukoumathes on a plate and sprinkle each stacked layer with warm honey, cinnamon, and walnuts. Serve hot with a side of vanilla ice cream.

Banana-Chocolate Loukoumathes

- Cut a small banana slice and place in the center of each ball of batter before frying them. When serving cooked banana loukoumathes, drizzle with chocolate syrup, honey and nuts. Serve with side of chocolate and vanilla frozen yogurt or ice cream.

Glossary

Seasoning
Herbs, spices, salt, and pepper are common ingredients used to give food extra flavor.

Marinating
Soaking food in a sauce before cooking makes food more tender and adds flavor.

Grilling
Cooking food quickly at a high temperature is what makes grilling unique. Grilling is typically done in an oven broiler, or on an outdoor grill.

Frying
To fry food means to cook it in oil or butter until it is crisp.

Baking
Cooking food in an oven is baking. Plan ahead, turn the oven on in advance to allow the oven time to warm before you begin baking.

Simmering
Cooking ingredients on a stove top at a heat level that allows the mixture to bubble.

Boiling
Cooking ingredients over high heat so that the mixture bubbles and steams.

Dicing
Cutting food into small cubes with a knife. To dice a vegetable, such as a carrot, cut it in half lengthwise, then cut into thin strips.

Chopping
Using a knife to cut food into smaller chunks. All cutting should be done safely on a cutting board. To chop herbs, group the stalks together and hold them down, then slice across in small strokes.

Slicing
Using a knife with a firm hand to create a steady, back and forth cut.

Pitting
Removing the stone or seeds from fruit. Using a knife, cut the fruit in half, following the crease down the side of the fruit.

Beating
Beating is a type of mixing, or stirring that can be done with a whisk or fork. For example, if a recipe calls for eggs to be beat – stir until the yolks and whites are mixed together.

Whisking
Using a whisk utensil, or electric mixer, whisking is a form of beating a liquid to create a complete mixture, or to create a thicker form – such as whip cream, or egg whites.

Folding In
Folding is a method of combing two things together by gently scooping the mixture, then turning it over and around inside a bowl until it is mixed evenly.

Sifting
Sifting is a shaking technique done with dry ingredients such as flour or sugar, and is easiest when using a tool called a sieve (similar to a strainer, but with a fine mesh). The goal of sifting is to remove lumps, and make the flour or sugar airy.

Greasing
Greasing a pan prevents food from sticking while cooking. Butter, oil, or lard can be used as a grease and rubbed lightly on a pan or oven proof dish. Alternatively, use cooking spray.

Creaming
To cream butter and sugar together, cut up softened butter and mix with a sugar in a bowl using a wooden spoon or solid cooking utensil.

Rolling Pastry Dough
Using a rolling pin, sprinkle a surface lightly with flour. Flatten a ball of dough with your hand, then use the rolling pin to roll dough flat by pressing firmly on the rolling pin and pushing the dough away from you.

About The Author

Stephanie Patsalis

Stephanie is a lover of food, family, friends, and living life to the fullest. As a young girl, her passion for food began in the Koroni, Greece kitchen of her beloved yiayia (Greek for grandmother). Asimina single-handedly instructed all of the younger generations to cook, passing down traditional family recipes and techniques from the Peloponnesus region. Now, Stephanie is an experienced food entrepreneur and talented business person. She is a visionary and a big picture thinker, especially when it comes to sharing her love of Mediterranean cuisine.

She authored the Greek Chic Cuisine cookbook, recorded a culinary DVD and a created a line of gourmet food products. She enjoys speaking and teaching culinary classes based on the Mediterranean Diet at Whole Foods Market, schools, and corporate and community events, such as South Beach Food and Wine Festival.

While her love of traditional family recipes continues, she enjoys creating new Mediterranean inspired healthy recipes for culinary classes, demonstrations and events. She presently serves on Red Brik Road Foundation, a non-profit dedicated to fostering awareness among children and families about the benefits of Mediterranean foods, nutrition and health and promoting the advancement of culinary careers. Stephanie is a second generation Greek American, a world traveler and mother to two daughters, Athena and Eleni.

Made in the USA
Middletown, DE
21 October 2020

ATHENA to ZEUS

A–Z of Mediterranean Cooking

A playbook of hands-on-fun recipes, the Athena to Zeus cookbook is merely the beginning of a sensory exploration into the world of fresh ingredients. By summoning the senses of smell, touch, and taste, the reader becomes a culinary creator and inventor, embarking on an adventure that can be savored as much in taste, as it is in the heart and mind.

We'll take you to the tippy top of Mount Olympus over the Greek Isles and into the hearts and minds of the Greek gods. Let this be your personal invitation to dig into culinary adventure. Gather your family for a cooking project! Whether you're in search of an appetizer for your next gathering, a main dish, a special Sunday morning breakfast, or dessert, you'll find a tasty recipe that's sure to be enjoyed by people of all ages, especially the young at heart.

Καλή όρεξη

www.athenatozeuscooking.com

ISBN 9780578775791

90000

9 780578 775791